PRAYERS

for the

No Longer Young

Introduction

Most of the prayers in this booklet were written by older people, many of them in their eighties. The prayers in the first section were collected by Mary C. White and first published by Forward Movement in 1979. For those writers, Mrs. White wrote, "God is not dead and they believe he can heal their hurts, help them over hurdles and show them how to avoid hazards." Additional prayers, beginning on page 60, from Canadian Anglicans, were collected by the Rev. Rollo M. Boas of British Columbia. The prayers are, he wrote, an expression of "what they believe about themselves and human nature and what they believe about God and all life."

Look with mercy, O God our Father, on all whose increasing years bring them weakness, distress, or isolation. Provide for them homes of dignity and peace; give them understanding helpers, and the willingness to accept help; and, as their strength diminishes, increase their faith and their assurance of your love. This we ask in the name of Jesus Christ our Lord. Amen.

CONTENTS

Retirement

God give me work till my life
    shall end
And life until my work is done.

                  (Source unknown)

O God, who numbers all our days,
Help us to find new paths
For a new time,
New friends in new places,
New thankfulness of heart
Through Jesus Christ our Lord.

              (Robert N. Rodenmayer)

RETIREMENT

Retirement can be a spiritual crisis of the first magnitude. If the central meaning of a person's life is business, titles, position and power, and if retirement strips him of these things, leaving him spiritually empty or naked, that is a spiritual crisis and some people die quickly. Instead of seeing himself as a child of God and a pilgrim, he sees himself as a has-been and stands at the abyss gazing into nothingness. Man without God is not man. His stability is not in himself nor in the shifting sands of this earth, but is derived from his relationship to God.

If you wish to retire well, do not

look upon yourself at center as a businessman, a biologist, or a bishop; see yourself, rather, as a child of God who happens to be serving God in these fields. Then in all the changes there will be a unity, and in all the ups and downs, a stability.

(Richard S.M. Emrich)

PSALM 32:8

You are my hiding-place; you preserve me from trouble; you surround me with shouts of deliverance.

ACCEPTING CHANGE

O Lord my God, who hast blessed me far beyond my merit or desert, I praise thee that thou hast given me the further gift of long life and enabled me to retire from the more strenuous activities of a working life. Now open to me, I pray, other avenues of service to thee and my fellowmen and give me the desire to accept these opportunities that thou hast set before me. Keep me alert to the fact that my advancing years will mean diminishing strength of body and mind. Help me to keep my mind open to new ideas, so that I may resist the temptation of living in the past and of trying to force old ideas on those who must make decisions in this ever-changing present.

Let me face the future without fear, in the knowledge that thou will sustain me by thy grace in whatever will befall me. When my time comes to enter the gates of larger life, if so in thy love it may be, let it be with a measure of swiftness and dignity; giving me time to thank thee for the love of my dear wife, of my family, of my friends and former colleagues, as well as time to repent of my many sins, and to receive the blessed assurance of thy forgiveness which thou hast given to thy servants in the commission of thy Son, my Lord and Savior.

(Leland W.F. Stark)

LIVING EACH DAY

Dear Lord and Father of us all, help us to live this final chapter of our lives with quiet fortitude, accepting the fact that we are dispensable but believing that we can still contribute in many ways to the quality of life for others.

Keep us from dwelling in the past. There are memories that bless, but there are also those that hurt. Help us to live each day for itself, with the gospel of love taught us by Thy Son Jesus Christ to guide us. Thou hast given us the gift of life and this beautiful world in which to live. Limited by age in our activities, nevertheless we can show by word and deed our faith in Thee and our caring for all humanity.

In Christ's name we pray. Amen.

(Dorothy Pugh)

PSALM 13:5-6

But I put my trust in your mercy; my heart is joyful because of your saving help. I will sing to the LORD, for he has dealt with me richly; I will praise the Name of the Lord Most High.

FOR PATIENCE

Heavenly Father, I come before you today asking for patience to deal with my dear one who finds it very hard to face retirement. He does not realize that my work in the home continues and that there are daily tasks to be performed. Help me to think of ways in which he can help me. May I never by word or deed cause him to feel he is under my feet and that I wish he could be able to go to work as usual. Yes Lord, I need an abundance of patience!

(Rita Hogan)

2 A.M. Tossing and Turning

Make Peace with Wakefulness

(Pier Macusi-Ungaro)

O Lord, let me sleep! You have said that you would give your beloved sleep. I know you love me; please give me sleep. Or let me rest quietly in you and realize that I am sharing with you the sleeplessness of the starving, the lonely, the lost and the old who are much worse off than I.

(Etta A. Gullich)

From ONE WHO LISTENS.
Copyright by Morehouse-Barlow.
Used by permission.

I SHOULD NOT COMPLAIN

I am not going to attempt to pray for long now, Lord, or it will keep me awake even more. All I want to say is that I accept this sleeplessness and unite it to what you suffered on the night of Thursday in Holy Week. I am at least resting and more or less comfortable. You were allowed no moment of rest, no shred of comfort. Often I have deliberately stayed awake at night for reasons of pleasure and not particularly complained afterwards. Tonight I can make my involuntary wakefulness an act of love. In which case I must certainly not complain afterwards. And now if it is your will, let me sleep. But if it is not, it does not matter.

(Dom Hubert van Zeller)

from WORKING WHILE YOU PRAY.
Copyright by Burns & Oates, London.
Used by permission.

THE GREAT GIFT OF SLEEP

O God who hast drawn over weary day the restful veil of night, enfold us in thy heavenly peace. Lift from our hands the weight of our burdens and sorrows. For untroubled slumber may we press our weakness close to thy strength and win power from thee, who gavest us the great gift of sleep.

(Source unknown)

THE COMFORTING RADIO

Almighty God, creator of the universe, through the ages thou hast given to countless others the power also to create. I thank thee for the miracle of the radio that when I cannot sleep brings me music and faceless voices that talk to me, making me think of others rather than of myself.

I thank thee, too, for the darkness that comes after the hassle of the day, and for the clear nights when the stars twinkle and the moon shines.

But most of all for sleep that finally comes, giving me rest and making it possible to meet the problems of tomorrow with a clear mind.   (Mary C. White)

Inevitable Changes

When white hair comes, I will carry you still—Will carry you and bring you to safety.

(Isaiah 46:4)

O Lord, don't let anything come my way today that you and I can't handle.

(A Tibetan Prayer)

THIS IS ANOTHER DAY

This is another day, O Lord. I
know not what it will bring
forth,

but make me ready, Lord, for
whatever it may be.

If I am to stand up, help me to
stand bravely.

If I am to sit still, help me to sit
quietly.

If I am to lie low, or to do nothing, help me to do it pa-
tiently...

Make these words more than
words and give me this Spirit
of Jesus.

(American Book of
Common Prayer,
p. 461, adapted)

AS I GROW OLD

As I grow old, God keep my
   heart attuned to laughter.
When youth is gone,
when all the days are gray days,
Coming after the sun and
   warmth,
God keep me from bitterness
   and grieving
When life seems cold.
God keep me always loving and
   believing
As I grow old.

(Source unknown)

I LIVE ALONE

I live alone, dear Lord, stay by
    my side,
In all my daily needs be thou my
    guide.
Grant me good health, for that
    indeed I pray
To carry on my work from day to
    day.
Keep pure my mind, my
    thoughts, my every deed;
Let me be kind, unselfish in my
    neighbor's need.
Spare me from fire, flood, mali-
    cious tongues,
From thieves, from fear and evil
    ones.
If sickness or accident befall,
Then, Lord, hear thou my
    humble call.

And when I'm feeling low or in
    despair,
Lift up my heart and help me in
    my prayer.
I live alone, Lord, but have no fear,
Because I feel thy presence ever
    near.

(Source unknown)

PSALM 25:6

Remember not the sins of my youth and my transgressions; remember me according to your love and for the sake of your goodness, O LORD.

KEEP ME STILL VALUABLE

Heavenly Father, I come with eyes growing dim, with limbs failing in strength, with my spirit full of despair. I can no longer see a purpose for my life. Show me Lord that you need me, that people as well as things can be valuable when they are old. Reassure me that I am valuable in thy sight, Lord, and so can bring to others life abundant.

(Walter E. Lewis)

ABIDING IN GOD'S LOVE

Lord, I believe that if we abide in your love, "the best is yet to be" no matter what our age. As I begin this new day, give me the grace and wisdom to live every moment in the knowledge that you are leading me step by step into that joy that you have prepared for all who unfeignedly love you. This I ask in his name, my Savior, Jesus Christ. Amen.

(Carroll E. Simcox)

PRAYER FOR MY MATURE YEARS

Today I celebrate our convenant
of life, O my Father:
  grateful that I am alive
  humbled that I am loved by you
  joyous that I can love in return.

Accept my daily offering
  for moments of surprise and
    wonder which opened up
    the common place
  for feelings of harmony that
    have made designs in my
    fragments
  for equanimity which has
    ordered my confusion
  for new loves who have
    peopled my loneliness

for your strength which has
   dispelled my terror of help-
   lessness.
Lead me in our celebration of the
covenant of life to that pinnacle
where I renew life in all its tenses.
But, help me to live in the present,
today, within the circle of your love
and its promise for the morrow.

(Robert S. Balfe)

AFTER EIGHTY

Is everything far bigger than of old
Far quicker and far noisier in its
    pace?
So let it be, yet in my heart I know
That slow and small and quiet
    things yet live
And on their gentler motions go
And from their store I still may
    take—and give.

(Mark DeWolfe Howe)

FORGETTING OUR PAINS

O God, when I think of thee I forget my aches and pains. Fill my mind with cares and concerns so great that they will crowd out my little complaints. Help me to accept my physical limitations and take them without wishing I were made in a different way. Thou hast made me as I am and I have not always done the best I could with what I have. Let me always remember what I have come through. If I must miss things that other people seem to enjoy, help me to let them go, without losing either my gladness or my love.

(Theodore Parker Ferris)

Permission of Trinity Church, Boston

I'M LOSING MY LOOKS

Oh, God, dear God, I'm showing my age. I'm not young and beautiful anymore the way my heart imagines. When I look in the mirror I could cry. For I look just what I am—a woman growing older. And I protest it Lord. Perhaps foolishly, I am stricken.

"Vanity, vanity, all is vanity," the Bible says. But is vanity truly such a fault? You, who made women with this instinctive hunger to hang onto personal beauty, must surely understand. Dear God, if this be vanity, let me use it to some good purpose.

Let it inspire me to keep my body strong and well and agile, the way you made it in the beginning. May it help me to stay as attractive as possible for as long as possible—out of concern for other people as well as myself. For you, who made women, also know that when we feel attractive we're a lot easier to live with.

But oh God, whatever happens to my face and body, keep me always supple in spirit, resilient to new ideas, beautiful in the things I say and do. If I must "show my age" let it be in some deeper dimension of beauty that is ageless and eternal, and can only come from you.

Don't let me be so afraid of aging, God. Let me rejoice and reach out to be replenished; I know that each day I can be reborn into strength and beauty through you.

(Marjorie Holmes)

From I'VE GOT TO TALK TO
SOMEONE, GOD.
Published by Doubleday and Company.
Used with permission.

PSALM 31:1-3

In you, O LORD, have I taken refuge; let me never be put to shame; deliver me in your righteousness. Incline your ear to me; make haste to deliver me. Be my strong rock, a castle to keep me safe, for you are my crag and my stronghold; for the sake of your Name, lead me and guide me.

IN A NURSING HOME

Give O Lord thy compassionate understanding to us who can no longer care for ourselves. Be present within my heart here in this nursing home. I have lost my independence but gained security and have taken from my family and friends any further cause to worry about me. Keep me from making unnecessary demands upon the nurses and from being dreary when people come to see me. Guide me in finding ways in which I can help those around me. When my strength decreases and my limitations increase, grant me release from frustrations by finding other useful ways to serve thee. (Mary C. White)

TO SEE MORE CLEARLY

Dear Lord, we were taught in our youth to have high aspirations and to work hard to achieve them. Help us to realize that in our old age, with declining strength and energy, we can no longer carry the responsibilities and burdens we once did; and help us to be content with smaller achievements.

We thank thee for small and quiet things: the heady wine of a cool summer day; a rainy day; and a cold snowy one with its beauty making it a luxury to stay indoors. Show us how to have tranquility of mind and spirit in spite of reduced capabilities, that we may be at peace with ourselves and with the world around us. Then as Jesus Christ has taught us, we may devote our thoughts and the fruits of our experience to helping others.

(Robert Oley)

THE QUICKENING NEW, THE SUSTAINING OLD

Oh God, who dost quicken us by the new and sustain us by the old, grant that the old may be freshened by the new and the new deepened by the old through him who is the same yesterday, today and forever.

(Roland A. Bainton)

COPING WITH BAD HABITS

Lord, thou knowest better than I know myself that I am growing older and will soon be old. Keep me from the fatal habit of thinking I must say something on every subject and on every occasion. Release me from craving to straighten out everyone's affairs. Make me thoughtful but not moody, helpful but not bossy. With my store of wisdom it seems a pity not to use it all, but thou knowest Lord I want to have a few friends in the end. Keep my mind from the endless recital of details, give me wings to get to the point. Seal my lips on my aches and pains. They are increasing and the love of rehearsing them is becoming sweeter as the years go by. I dare not ask for grace enough to enjoy the tales of others, but help me to endure them with patience. I do not ask for improved memory but a growing humility and a lessening cocksureness when my memory seems to clash with the memory of others. Teach me the glorious lesson that sometimes I may be mistaken. Keep me reasonably sweet. I do not want to be a saint (some of them are so hard to live with), but a sour old person is the crowning work of the devil. Give me the ability to see good in unexpected places and talents in unexpected persons. Give me the grace to tell them so.

(Source unknown)

ON CARRYING CROSSES

Almighty God, we know that you do not deliberately cause us to suffer but that you do enable us to carry our burdens. Grant that we may do so with grace. There is so much pain in the world, there is so much self-pity in our hearts, that we are tempted to forget you because it seems as though you had forgotten us. Keep us from doing this by keeping ever before us the figure of your Son, Jesus Christ, the way he carried his cross, and the power that you brought into the world by his resurrection. So we offer with him now the pain that is ours, the agony of indecision, the suspicion of betrayal, the fear that we may do wrong because we are wrong, the responsibilities for which we seem inadequate. We remember that whatever you ask us to do, you help us do it. May we in the light of Christ's victory be strengthened to go on with a lighter step, a renewed sense of purpose, and a vision of the goodness and wholeness that may be ours.

(John B. Coburn)

From A DIARY OF PRAYERS—
PERSONAL AND PUBLIC.
Copyright ©1975
by The Westminister Press.

BEDRIDDEN

Shut up in this little room, surrounded by those four bare walls, keep me, O Lord, from feeling cut off from life. Let the air I breathe and the light I see be the signs to me of the Life that comes in from outside. Let the kindness that surrounds me and the care that never lets me go be the center of a world too big to cramp me and too good to blot me out.

(Theodore Parker Ferris)

Permission of Trinity Church, Boston

DIVINE ALCHEMY

O Lord, Creator, grant to us who are hurt or sick in mind, body or spirit the sure knowledge that it is you we can seek and find and to you we can cling. May we realize that through the divine alchemy of your love we can walk with you and delight in you, through him that made the lame walk, the blind see and the deaf hear, even thy Son Jesus Christ, minister, teacher, physician and friend.

(Nan Day)

LORD, I'VE HAD ENOUGH

Lord today I've had enough. It just doesn't make sense for me to go on. My old friends are all gone. I can't do anything except be a burden to people and this old body just aches and pains, my mind slips, I can't remember what I'm doing or even what day it is. Lord I've had enough. Couldn't you take me?

*****

My child, I know you hurt and that you want to come home. Be patient, I will bring you home. You still have a gift for this world; how you live these special last days shows the people about you that you are in my hands. You can count on me just as Jesus did when he had had enough and put himself in my hands.

*****

I'll try, Lord.

(Frederick Warnecke Jr.)

PSALM 9:1-2

I will give thanks to you, O LORD, with my whole heart; I will tell of all your marvelous works. I will be glad and rejoice in you; I will sing to your Name, O Most High.

CATARACTS

Lord we thank thee for the miracles of modern medicine, so that cataracts that once meant blindness can in many cases be removed. Save us from impatience with the slow and incomplete results. When the barriers are gone, we rejoice in the beautiful colors we can see again; help us to remember that joy when later we chafe at our inability to see objects in clear definition. When we get our new glasses, we are grateful for how clearly we see; keep us thankful when later we realize how limited our peripheral vision may be. Help us not only to give thanks for our blessings but

to accept gracefully those handi-
caps that cannot be overcome.

(Robert Oley)

PSALM 46:1-4

God is our refuge and strength, a
very present help in trouble.
Therefore we will not fear, though
the earth be moved, and though
the mountains be toppled into the
depths of the sea; Though its wa-
ters rage and foam, and though
the mountains tremble at its tu-
mult. The LORD of hosts is with us;
the God of Jacob is our stronghold.

IF I HAD MY LIFE
TO LIVE OVER

I'd dare to make more mistakes
next time. I'd relax. I would
limber up.

I would be sillier than I have
this trip. I would take fewer
things seriously.

I would take more chances. I
would take more trips.

I would climb more mountains
and swim more rivers.

I would eat more ice cream and
less beans.

I would perhaps have more ac-
tual troubles, but I'd have
fewer imaginary ones.

You see, I'm one of those people
who live sensibly and sanely
hour after hour, day after day.

Oh, I've had my moments and if
I had it to do over again, I'd
have more of them.
In fact, I'd try to have nothing
else.
Just moments, one after another, instead of living so
many years ahead of each
day.
I've been one of those persons
who never goes anywhere
without a thermometer, hot
water bottle, a raincoat and a
parachute.
If I had it to do again, I would
travel lighter than I have.
If I had my life to live over,
I would start barefoot earlier in
the spring and stay that way
later in the fall.

I would go to more dances.
I would ride more merry-go-
rounds.
I would pick more daisies.

(Nadine Stair)

PSALM 12:7

O LORD, watch over us and save us from this generation for ever.

PSALM 4:7-8

You have put gladness in my heart, more than when grain and wine and oil increase. I lie down in peace; at once I fall asleep; for only you, LORD, make me dwell in safety.

Losing Our Dear Ones

The human spirit though it may be bruised and crushed is indestructible.

(A.J. Cronin)

They will come back—come back again—
As long as the red Earth rolls,
He never wasted a leaf or a tree.
Do you think he would squander souls?

(Rudyard Kipling)

THE BEYOND

What lies beyond the grave we
    do not know,
Would that our loved ones could
    return and tell;
We can but carry on and wait
Till after the tolling of the bell.
But even now we feel a power
    astir.
The resurrection can take place
    within.
And though there is no voice
    from out the cloud,
We sense a presence and are
    cleansed from sin.

                (Roland A. Bainton)

GOD OF THE DESOLATE

O God of all the desolate
Hear thy people cry,
Some die for honor, love and
　　truth
And some just simply die.
We know not why this all should
　　be,
Our faith is sorely tried,
We hope we have a clue in thee,
In Christ the crucified.

(Roland A. Bainton)

LIFE AS A GIFT

Teach me, O Lord, not to hold onto life too tightly. Teach me to hold it lightly, not carelessly, but lightly, easily. Teach me to take it as a gift to enjoy and to cherish while I have it, and let it go gracefully and thankfully when the time comes. The gift is great, but the giver is greater still. Thou O God are the Giver, and in thee is life that never dies.

(Theodore Parker Ferris)

Permission of Trinity Church, Boston

LIFE ETERNAL, LOVE IMMORTAL

We seem to give them back to thee, dear God, who gavest them to us. Yet as thou didst not lose them in giving, so we have not lost them by their return . . . For what is thine is ours always if we are thine. And life is eternal; and love is immortal; and death is only a horizon; and a horizon is nothing save the limit of our sight. Lift us up, strong Son of God, that we may see further; cleanse our eyes that we may see more clearly; draw us closer to thyself that we may know ourselves nearer to our beloved who are with thee . . . that where they are and thou art, we too may be.   (Source unknown)

FOR THOSE LOVED BUT LOST

O Father of all, we pray to thee for those we love, but see no longer. Grant them thy peace; let light perpetual shine upon them; and in thy loving wisdom and almighty power work in them the good purpose of thy perfect will.

(Forward Movement
Publications)

AT THE LAST AWAKENING

Bring us, O Lord, at our last awakening into the house and gate of heaven, to enter into that gate and dwell in that house where there shall be no darkness but one equal light, no noise or silence but one equal music, no fears and hopes but one equal eternity in the habitation of thy glory and dominion, world without end.

(John Donne)

Additional Prayers

IN THE EVENING OF LIFE

O Lord Jesus Christ, we pray Thee abide with all Thy people in the evening of life. Make Thyself known to them, and let Thy light shine upon their path, and whenever they shall pass through the valley of the shadow of death, be with them through and beyond.

(Submitted by Dora Cliffe)

PSALM 22:18

Be not far away, O LORD; you are my strength; hasten to help me.

TOUCHING LIVES

All through this day,
O Lord,
Let me touch as many lives as
    possible
For thee.
And every life I touch, do thou
By thy Holy Spirit
Quicken,
Whether through the
Word I speak, the
prayer I breathe, the
Letters I write, or the
Life I live.

(Submitted by
Nancy McArton)

WHEN OUR HEALTH IS FAILING

Most Merciful Father, with a deep sense of gratitude, we thank you for the balance of health we have enjoyed for most of our lives. We understand that in our later years, our bodies gradually begin to slow down. Our minds too become less able to cope with the myriad of things we are expected to remember. Help us, Lord, to accept these changes, and to deal with them to the best of our ability. We also ask for your spiritual strength during periods of ill health to endure what we must, gracefully. Make us aware that there are others whose pain may be greater than our own. May your love shine through our discomfort, and give us the faith to put our whole trust in you.

(Florence E. Bremner)

I TURNED AWAY

Forgive me, Lord; I turned away from someone today. I didn't think they would understand me, or what growing older is like, or how life has treated me. Aging has made me less tolerant towards others. My lack of understanding, and my daily frustrations blind me; I'm sorry if I hurt people, Lord. I'm sorry I turned away from you today.

(Peter J. Slade)

UNTIL THE TIME OF TRANSITION

O Lord, may we feel your presence more deeply, enriching the advancing years until the time of transition, when we no longer need the earthly body and you bid us cast it away. May we do this without anger or resentment but with grace and acceptance, in the knowledge that you are always with us. And, O Lord God, we pray that we shall not be empty-handed as you raise us into new life.

(Lorna Nesbitt)

THE NEW DAY

Father, I thank Thee for another sunrise, for a new day with new opportunities. Grant me the will, the strength, the awareness to care for someone as you care for me. Strengthen me to commit my life to you by serving one of your children who is in need. Grant that my discomfort will diminish and my joy in your service increase, as I am fortunate to complete another day in your creation, for we do all in the name of Him who first lived the way.

(Colmar Russell)

FOR FAMILY

Lord Jesus, I pray for my family, for my children and my children's children. Let us not be burdens to one another so much as a joy, help and hope for the years to come. Give us closeness and love, and a sense of your presence, that we may come together and find our common ground in you, Lord.

(Peter J. Slade)

PSALM 8:5-6

What is man that you should be mindful of him? the son of man that you should seek him out?

IN THE LIFE TO COME

Lord Jesus touch me; show me that I matter and that you care. Those I love are dying to this life, and I feel so alone. Strengthen my faith, Lord, and give me hope, that in the life to come, I too, may rise to new life.

(Peter J. Slade)

May our sunsets be bright and happy, until we arrive at that glorious sunrise, our eternal home.

(Ann Wilson)

Someone recently said: I just sit quietly and talk to God, repeating "I love you, God."

(P.C. Daly)

"PETER, WHEN YOU ARE OLD"

God, I have so much to offer,
    but my age has sidelined me;
I have experienced so much of life
    but that was "then", not "now";
They think I cannot change my
    ways,
    because my body is too old;
If I must become yet again as a
    child,
    ruled by the will of others,
    made to go places I don't
    want to,
    made to do things I'd rather
    not,
Lord, please do not desert me;
You may be all I have left.

              (Peter J. Slade)

CELEBRATING MY YEARS

Lord, help me to celebrate my years. Help me to feel good about myself. Help me to forgive others who just don't understand. Let me keep loving, giving and caring. Help me to be more like you.

(Peter J. Slade)

PSALM 22:29-30

My soul shall live for him; my descendants shall serve him; they shall be known as the LORD'S for ever. They shall come and make known to a people yet unborn the saving deeds that he has done.

PAYING ATTENTION

Keep me mindful, Lord,
   throughout this day of the
   prayers I have said,
   and those for whom I've
   prayed.
Keep me in good spirits:
   vigorous and curious and
   humorous;
   ready always with laughter,
   with passion and with tears;
prompt to see the seriousness of
   light matters, the lightness of
   serious ones, and myself as
   the least serious matter of all.

                    (T.D. Stewart)

HEALING PEACE

Lord God, Lamb of God, you take
Away the sins of the world,
Grant us peace.
Peace in my soul and my body,
As tonight I give you all
My hurts and frustrations of
    today,
And give myself to you in sleep.
Give to me, O Lord, as I rest
In you, your forgiveness too.

                    (Caroline McLean)

FOR OUR PARENTS AND GRANDPARENTS

Father, Lord God, Almighty King, we graciously thank you for our parents, our grandparents and all those who came before us. We thank you for all their gifts which you have so generously bestowed upon them. We thank you for: their strength, when we had none; their courage, when our hearts failed us; their perseverance, when we left the road; their wisdom, when we needed counsel; their love, when we were alone; their forgiveness, when we erred. May we ask you for blessing of health and peace for our parents during their final years. For those in illness and infirmity, may we be pillars of strength against which they may lean. Above all, when we are parents and grand-parents, may we give in the same way to our children as our parents have given to us.

(Alice Nowosielski)

O Lord, support us all the day long of this troublous life, until the shadows lengthen and the evening comes, the busy world is hushed, the fever of life is over, and our work is done. Then, in Thy mercy, grant us safe lodging, and a holy rest and peace at the last.

(John Henry Newman)

GOING HOME

There comes a time when the most hard-bitten retiree is likely to realize that the classical Christian statement, "earthly life is a time for soul-making," expresses sense-making truth. Two truths, in fact: that God has prepared for us exiles from Eden a permanent home where dwells his Son, the gracious Person for whom the human soul insatiably longs; and that God has also provided a home away from home where we first meet and come to know him.

I don't know the physical geography, if any, of our eternal homeland. Life is process, not edifice, anyway. But I am confident that when we emerge from the long dark tunnel under our final sunset Mountain and burst out to see it spread before us we'll recognize it, with deep satisfaction and sure knowledge, to be home. The conditions of life here will have prepared us for the continuous, everlasting, conditions of life there.

(Gale Webb)

PSALM 62:1-2

For God alone my soul in silence waits; from him comes my salvation. He alone is my rock and my salvation, my stronghold, so that I shall not be greatly shaken.

PSALM 16:5-11

O LORD, you are my portion and my cup; it is you who uphold my lot. My boundaries enclose a pleasant land; indeed, I have a goodly heritage. I will bless the LORD who gives me counsel; my heart teaches me, night after night. I have set the LORD always before me; because he is at my right hand I shall not fall. My heart, therefore, is glad, and my spirit rejoices; my body also shall rest in hope. For you will not abandon me to the grave, nor let your holy one see the Pit. You will show me the path of life; in your presence there is fullness of joy, and in your right hand are pleasures for evermore.